A DISCUSSION G

#1 NATIONAL

THE PAGAN CHRIST

"Read this book . . . to enrich your personal quest for truth in order to break through previously unchallenged boundaries of religious insularity and exclusivism . . . challenges complacency and opens new vistas of insight to the serious thinker." — *Toronto Star*

"A truly revolutionary work, devout but subversive in the best sense, with a carefully constructed narrative that challenges believers and non-believers to fundamentally re-examine 'the Greatest Story Ever Told' . . . a dramatic conclusion, firmly held and well detailed." — *Edmonton Journal*

"Provocative? You bet! Harpur's book is guaranteed to antagonize conservative belief in the Bible as God's literal word, but ecumenical enthusiasts will delight in its message." — *Shared Vision*

Books of Merit

TOM HARPUR

RECOVERING THE LOST LIGHT

THE PAGAN CHRIST

A DISCUSSION GUIDE

Introduction by Tom Harpur

Thomas Allen Publishers
Toronto

Library and Archives Canada Cataloguing in Publication

The pagan Christ : recovering the lost light. Discussion guide.

Supplement to: Pagan Christ.
ISBN 0-88762-169-4

1. Christianity—Origin. 2. Christianity and other religions.
3. Church history—Primitive and early church, ca. 30–600.

BR129.H37 2004 SUPPL   270.1   C2004-903480-4

Questions compiled by Rev. Larry Marshall
Text design: Sharon Foster
Cover image: Max Kandhola/Photonica

Published by Thomas Allen Publishers,
a division of Thomas Allen & Son Limited
145 Front Street East, Suite 209
Toronto ON M5A 1E3 Canada

www.thomas-allen.com

**Canada Council
for the Arts**

ONTARIO ARTS COUNCIL
CONSEIL DES ARTS DE L'ONTARIO

The publisher gratefully acknowledges the support of
the Ontario Arts Council for its publishing program.

We acknowledge the support of the Canada Council for the Arts, which
last year invested $21.7 million in writing and publishing throughout Canada.

We acknowledge the Government of Ontario through the
Ontario Media Development Corporation's Ontario Book Initiative.

We acknowledge the financial support of the government of Canada
through the Book Publishing Industry Development Program (BPIDP)
for our publishing activities.

08 07 06 05 04   1 2 3 4 5

Printed and bound in Canada

"The Jesus of Nazareth who came forward publicly as the Messiah, who preached the ethic of the Kingdom of God, who founded the Kingdom of Heaven upon earth, and died to give his work its final consecration, never had any existence. He is a figure designed by rationalism, endowed with life by liberalism and clothed by modern theology in a historical garb."

— DR. ALBERT SCHWEITZER,
The Quest of the Historical Jesus

"The Imitatio Christi (the imitation of Christ) will forever have this disadvantage; we worship a man as a divine model, embodying the deepest meaning of life, and then out of sheer imitation we forget to make real the profound meaning present in ourselves . . . If I accept the fact that a god is absolute and beyond all human experience, he leaves me cold. I do not affect him, nor does he affect me. But if I know, on the other hand, that God is a mighty activity within my own soul, at once I must concern myself with him."

— CARL G. JUNG

"The very thing is now called the Christian religion existed among the ancients also, nor was it wanting from the inception of the human race until the coming of Christ in the flesh, at which point the true religion, which was already in existence, began to be called Christian."

— ST. AUGUSTINE, *Retractiones*

"But we have this treasure in earthen vessels."

— ST. PAUL, 2 Corinthians 4:7

"Do you not know that you are the temple of God, and that the Spirit of God dwells in you?"

— 1 Corinthians 3:16

"Though Christ a thousand times in Bethlehem be born,
But not within thyself, they soul will be forlorn;
The cross on Golgotha thou lookest to in vain
Unless within thyself it be set up again."

— ANGELUS SILESIUS

Introduction by Tom Harpur

"I don't know how to find the words to express the incredible joy, excitement, and peace that have descended upon me since reading *The Pagan Christ*. I feel as if a door of incredible opportunity has been opened for me (and for everyone) to find a more authentic, rational, and deeply spiritual faith. After completing a Masters degree in Religious Studies, I found it impossible to believe in Christianity any longer. This book has reopened the history of truth that I caught only a glimpse of during my graduate studies. It has explained so much, created many new questions, and opened up a whole new world of rational theological wonder. Thank you!"

— J.S., A READER

THIS LETTER IS but one of hundreds of very similar responses that I have already received and that continue to flood in as word of *The Pagan Christ* and its message continues to spread rapidly. Perhaps you, too, found your heart and mind resonating as you read this woman's deeply felt and very personal commentary. Let me welcome you as you prepare to explore more fully what she has rightly termed "a rational and deeply spiritual faith." Let me also share with you my profound conviction that in so doing you are part of what will one day be looked back upon as nothing less than the beginning of a rebirthing of the Christian religion for this new millennium. This enterprise is prompted and directed by the Divine Spirit — all around us and so intimately rooted in each of our beings. This is the same Spirit who makes all things new again.

We live in a time of great turmoil and upheaval. Old religious moorings have slipped into the darkness and vanished. At the same time, a myriad of voices on all sides clamor that they alone possess the only true way ahead. Confusion reigns. It is important to find and to work from a solid theological base — one that nevertheless is sufficiently universal and flexible to cope with fast-changing realities and a vastness of the cosmos that seems to expand as we draw each breath.

Having read *The Pagan Christ* through — perhaps more than once — is still only a beginning for those for whom it has already shed real light upon their spiritual journey. The discussions you are now about to embark upon will probe further into the significance of that light and hopefully enable you to open yourself up further to its meaning for your life.

We all owe a debt of gratitude to the Reverend Lawrence (Larry) Marshall for his devoted work in preparing this guide and for his leadership in the first official Toronto-based study group dedicated to pursuing these themes. Also, my thanks to editor Jim Gifford at Thomas Allen Publishers and to the publisher, Patrick Crean.

I invite you, then, to come to this discussion process in the sure knowledge that the Spirit of the Christ within every heart will guide you into all truth. A true adventure awaits you as you start out. You are part of a new birthing of the faith in our times. May God's blessing be upon you and yours every step of the way.

—Tom Harpur

CHAPTER ONE

Discovery: A Bible Story I'd Never Heard Before

"My point, once again, is not that those ancient people told literal stories and we are now smart enough to take them symbolically, but that they told them symbolically and we are now dumb enough to take them literally."

— JOHN DOMINIC CROSSAN, *Who Is Jesus?*

Begin by introducing yourselves and answering this question: *Where are you in your spiritual journey right now?*

good first question

1. What was your first impression on reading the title *The Pagan Christ*?

2. What is the meaning of the word "pagan"?

3. What "fatal and fateful error" did the church make in the third and fourth centuries?

4. What effect does the allegorical approach to the Bible have on you?

5. What do you think of pagan religion as being "foreshadowings" of Jesus? What does Harpur think?

6. How do you respond to the "startling new truth" that Harpur says we are about to encounter?

7. Discuss the following quote by Richard Holloway: "The end of Christianity is coming because there is a system undergirding the traditional economy of salvation which is more concerned with preserving its own power than exploring the truth."

8. How did the church of the fourth and fifth centuries handle the pagan sources of Christianity's doctrines, dogmas, and rites? How do you think they should have handled it?

9. What does Harpur believe will be the consequences of the "surgery" performed on Christianity?

10. What do you think the consequences will be? Why?

CHAPTER TWO

Setting the Stage:
Myths Aren't Fairy Tales

"On the intellectual side of religion and spirituality we are still dwelling in the lingering shadows of medieval night, hypnotized and victimized by superstition of the weirdest types flaunted from pulpit and seminary. This beclouded day of gloom will continue as long as we have not the acumen to dissociate sublime myth, allegory, drama and symbol from the dregs of history."

— ALVIN BOYD KUHN, *Who Is This King of Glory?*

Begin by answering this question: *What are the obstacles blocking your spiritual life and journey?*

1. What has been your understanding of myth?

2. What, according to Harpur, is the true meaning of myth?

3. Harpur believes that myth is better than history at expressing truth. Do you agree or disagree?

4. Discuss Harpur's assertion that <u>Christianity</u> does not need to de-mythologize its story, but that it <u>needs to re-mythologize it.</u>

5. How did the ancients use myth?

6. <u>Does belief in a flesh and blood redeemer distort Christianity</u> <u>for you?</u>

a circle quote

7. What does Harpur believe is the central theme of all religion?

8. Why was nature so important to the ancients?

9. What is a mystery play and how were they used?

10. Do you believe, as some scholars do, that in the long past ages there was one religion, a primal religion, that was the source of all religions?

11. Where did the brilliant insights and convictions of the ancients come from?

12. Discuss Harpur's summary of the spiritual Christ. How does this appeal to you?

CHAPTER THREE

Christianity before Christianity: Where It All Began

"The very thing which is now called the Christian religion existed among the ancients also, nor was it wanting from the inception of the human race until the coming of Christ in the flesh, at which point the true religion which was already in existence began to be called Christian."

— ST. AUGUSTINE, *Retractiones*

Begin by answering this question: *What concerns you most about Christianity?*

1. Share your reactions to the astounding statements of Augustine, Eusebius, Justin Martyr, Celsus, and Ammonius Saccas.

2. What are the parallels between Christianity and Buddhism?

3. According to Harpur, what is the core belief of all religions?

4. What is the crucial difference between the ancient myths and orthodox Christianity?

5. What is heresy and how was it used? Do you consider yourself a heretic?

6. What is the central story of every traditional faith?

7. Compare the Osiris-Dionysius myth with the story of Jesus.

8. What do you think is the only difference between the traditional Jesus story and other ancient myths?

9. What do you believe about the "second coming"? What does Harpur believe?

10. Harpur writes that each person has his or her own personal Christmas and Easter. Share your Christmas and Easter experiences.

11. What was the meaning of the cross millennia before Christianity?

12. What does the cross mean to you personally?

CHAPTER FOUR

The Greatest Cover-Up of All Time: How a Spiritual Christianity Became a Literalist Christianism

"There are many things that are true which is not useful for the vulgar crowd to know; and certain things which although they are false it is expedient for the people to believe otherwise."

— ST. AUGUSTINE, *City of God*

Begin by answering this question: *What concerns you most about the church?*

1. What is "Christianism"?

2. What caused Christianism?

3. What shocking charges can be made against the church fathers?

4. How did the church fathers justify these "pious frauds"? How do you react to the charge of pious fraud?

5. Who "corrected" the gospels and the writings of the church fathers?

6. How were the gospels corrected?

7. What priceless books were destroyed by the orders of the church?

8. What other destruction was caused by Christian fury?

9. Who was Hypatia and what happened to her?

10. What do you think of the church's charge to the pagans of "anticipated plagiarism"?

11. What is the Theodosian Code?

12. When did Plato's Academy in Athens finally close, and why?

13. What learned father of the church was excommunicated? Why?

14. What does Harpur believe the church should do now?

15. What do you believe the church should do now?

CHAPTER FIVE

It Was All Written Before — in Egypt

Part I: Ancient Egyptian Religion

Part II: Horus and Jesus

"All that went into the making of the Christian historical set-up was long pre-extant as something quite other than history, was in fact expressly non-historical, in the Egyptian mythology and eschatology. For when the sun at the Easter equinox entered the sign of the fishes (Pisces) about 255 B.C.E., the Jesus who stands as the founder of Christianity was at least [thousands] of years of age and had been travelling hither as the Ever Coming One through all preceding time . . . During those [millennia], that same incarnation of the divine ideal in the character of Iusa (or Horus), the Coming Son, had saturated the mind of Egypt with its exalting influence. Little did men of that epoch dream that their ideal figure of man's divinity would in time be rendered historical as a man of flesh."

— ALVIN BOYD KUHN, *Who Is This King of Glory?*

Begin by answering this question: *What changes would you like to see in Christianity?*

1. How is Osiris the prototype of Christ?

2. Why were Egyptian Christians so open to Christianity?

3. Does the story of Horus "touch" your life in any way?

4. What, according to Massey and Kuhn, is the origin of Matthew's name?

5. What is the Egyptian understanding of judgment and resurrection?

6. What was the hope of every Egyptian? What is your hope? Why?

7. What parallels exist between the stories of Horus and Jesus?

8. What does Harpur believe we need to discover and apply?

9. Who or what are the twelve disciples according to Kuhn and Massey?

10. What significance does the fish have for Christianity?

11. What is the true meaning of "only begotten"?

12. What details in the life of Jesus can be traced back to Egyptian religion?

CHAPTER SIX

Convincing the Sceptics

"The general assumption concerning the gospels is that the historic element was the kernel of the whole, and that fables accreted around it; whereas the myths, being pre-existent, prove that the core of the material was mythical, and it then follows that the "history" is incremental . . . The worst foes of the truth have ever been the rationalizers of the mythos. They have assumed the existence of a personal founder of Christianity as the fundamental fact. They have done their best to humanize . . . the mythos by discharging the supernatural and miraculous . . . in order that it might be accepted. Thus, they have lost the battle by fighting it on the wrong ground."

— GERALD MASSEY, *The Historical Jesus and the Mythical Christ*

Begin the discussion by answering this question: *What changes do you think the church should make right now?*

1. Do you think the church lost the battle? What does Massey say?

2. How does Harpur compare the births and baptisms of Horus and Jesus?

3. What is the allegorical interpretation of the temptation? Armageddon? Hell? Judgment?

4. What is the relevance of healing to our lives today?

5. What evidence is there that John was reworking Egyptian texts?

6. How was the Zodiac used by the ancients?

7. How was the fish used as a symbol for Christ?

8. What is the deeper meaning of Jesus' walking on the water?

9. What scriptures have Egyptian roots?

10. What kind of Christianity does Harpur believe is needed today? What kind of Christianity do you believe is needed today?

CHAPTER SEVEN

The Bible — History or Myth?: The End of Fundamentalism

"In the cosmic economy, the divine must always sacrifice its life for the lower ranks of existence. In every religion a god is pictured as dying for man."

— ALVIN BOYD KUHN, *Our Birth Is But a Sleep*

Begin by answering this question: *If the bible has little history in it what are the possible implications for the territory dispute between Israel and Palestine?*

1. How does the journalist Daniel Lazare pull "the foundations out from under almost every major historical beam in the edifice of accepted wisdom" with respect to the biblical patriarchs, the exodus, David and Solomon, and conquest of the promised land?

2. What evidence is there that the bible has little history in it?

3. How should we interpret the Old Testament stories of the exodus, Daniel, Samson, and Gideon?

4. What does Harpur say about the historical basis of the New Testament?

5. What deeper meaning does Harpur find in the parable of the prodigal son?

6. What puzzling aspects does Harpur raise about the Lazarus story?

7. How does he solve the puzzle?

8. What conclusions does Harpur come to with regard to the Lazarus event?

9. What meaning does the Lazarus story have for you?

10. Try your skills at interpreting allegorically the birth of Jesus, the miracles of Jesus, and the death and resurrection of Jesus.

CHAPTER EIGHT

Seeing the Gospels with New Eyes: Sublime Myth Is Not Biography

"The evidence suggests that the New Testament is not a history of actual events, but a history of the evolution of Christian mythology."

— TIMOTHY FREKE AND PETER GANDY, *The Jesus Mysteries*

"From a hoary civilization (Egypt) comes the literature that ends all debate by offering the incontrovertible evidence that the Gospels are not and never were histories. They are now proven to have been cryptic dramas of the spiritual evolution of humanity and of the history of the human soul in its earthly tabernacle of flesh."

— ALVIN BOYD KUHN, *Who Is This King of Glory?*

Begin by answering this question: *What particular Bible story puzzles you?*

1. How does Harpur believe the gospels came about?

2. What is the chief flaw of the Jesus Seminar according to Harpur?

3. What is the truth of the nativity for Harpur? What is truth of the nativity for you?

4. How does Harpur explain the passion of Jesus?

5. Why is the resurrection story suspect as a historical event?

6. What is the inner meaning of the resurrection?

7. Why was nature so important to ancient religions?

8. How does Harpur answer the question as to whether the gospels are true?

9. How were you taught to understand the gospels? How has your understanding changed?

10. Harpur believes that the Christ myth is the ultimate myth of the self. Does this understanding help you at all in gaining new meaning from the New Testament? Discuss.

CHAPTER NINE

Was There a Jesus of History?

"Jesus of Nazareth and the Gospel story cannot be found in Christian writings earlier than the Gospels, the first of which (Mark) was composed only in the late first century . . . There is no non-Christian record of Jesus before the second century."

— EARL DOHERTY, *The Jesus Puzzle*

"When the conception of a purely spiritual Christ could no longer successfully be imported to the turbulent masses, who clamored for a political saviour, it was found necessary or expedient to substitute the idea of a personal Messiah . . . The swell of this tide carried the Church Fathers to the limit of re-casting the entire four Gospels in terms of a human biography."

— ALVIN BOYD KUHN, *The Lost Light*

Begin by answering this question: *How would the non-historicity of Jesus affect you?*

1. Do you agree or disagree with Woody Allen's statement that God doesn't play dice with the universe but instead plays hide-and-seek?

2. What historical elements does Harpur believe are in the gospels?

3. What facts does Harpur assemble to prove the non-historicity of Jesus?

4. What are we to make of the references to Jesus in the works of Pliny, Tacitus, Seutonius, and Josephus?

5. What archetypal hero in the Old Testament was possibly the model for Jesus? Can you think of others? What about Psalm 22, or Isaiah 53?

6. What was Paul's understanding of Jesus?

7. What does Harpur make of Paul's conversion on the road to Damascus?

8. What words of Paul to King Agrippa prove that Paul's conversion was an inner experience?

9. What does a "personal Jesus" mean to you? Why is a personal Jesus not acceptable to Harpur? Is a personal Jesus acceptable to you?

10. What is the best proof of the "truth" of Christianity for you? What is the best proof according to Harpur?

CHAPTER TEN

The Only Way Ahead: Cosmic Christianity

"The historical Jesus as a civilizing influence has now been tried for nearly twenty centuries. With a weird irony, not only has it not in large measure elevated humanity in the West above an earlier barbarism, but it has in fact been used as a cloak for the worst atrocities and inhumanities that history records. The foulest cruelties were perpetrated in the very name of the gentle Nazarene! It well behooves humanity in the West to try the concept of the indwelling Christ, the hope of our glory."

— ALVIN BOYD KUHN, *The Root of All Religion*

Begin by answering the question: *What do you feel is the way ahead for each of you?*

1. How does the bible come alive for Harpur? Has it come alive for you?

2. Are you inspired with fresh hope? Is Harpur?

3. What symbols are clarified for Harpur?

4. What are the dangers of literalism?

5. What part did nature play in ancient religion?

6. What does the Jesus story mean to you?

7. If Christmas and Easter (or any other story in the Bible) are interpreted allegorically will they lose their power? Explain your answer.

8. Has your understanding of Christianity changed?

9. How has *The Pagan Christ* affected your faith?

10. What is your overall impression of *The Pagan Christ*?

11. How do you think this book will affect your faith? Your life?

BOOKS BY GERALD MASSEY

Ancient Egypt: The Light of the World
The Historical Jesus and the Mythical Christ
The Natural Genesis

RECOMMENDED READING

The Jesus Mysteries,
Timothy Freke and Peter Gandy

Jesus and the Lost Goddess,
Timothy Freke and Peter Gandy

The Gnostic Gospels, Elaine Pagels

The Gnostic Paul, Elaine Pagels

Beyond Belief, Elaine Pagels

The Bible Unearthed,
Israel Finkelstein and Neil Asher Silberman

Man and His Symbols, Carl G. Jung

The Masks of God, Joseph Campbell

Breakthrough, Matthew Fox

The Spiral Staircase, Karen Armstrong

The Runaway Bunny, Margaret Wise Brown

We hope you have enjoyed your
discussion of Tom Harpur's
The Pagan Christ: Recovering the Lost Light.

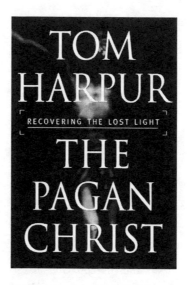

To order more copies of *The Pagan Christ*
or this discussion guide, check with your
local bookseller or call us at 1-800-387-4333
or fax us at 1-800-458-5504.

Please visit our web site for more information
of other Thomas Allen Publishers titles:

www.thomas-allen.com